WILLIAM SHAKESPEARE

120
SELECTED
POEMS

COLLECTABLE EDITION

120 SELECTED POEMS
COLLECTABLE EDITION
by WILLIAM SHAKESPEARE

Published by

Delhi Open Books

G/F, 4771/23, Bharat Ram Road, Daryaganj, New Delhi-110002
Ph.: 91-11-42408081
E-mail: delhiopenbooks2016@gmail.com

ISBN: 978-93-90997-22-0

Cover, Typesetting, and Book Design by **ROHIT**

William Shakespeare (bapt. 26 April 1564 – 23 April 1616)was an English playwright, poet, and actor, widely regarded as the greatest writer in the English language and the world's greatest dramatist.He is often called England's national poet and the "Bard of Avon" (or simply "the Bard").His extant works, including collaborations, consist of some 39 plays,154 sonnets, three long narrative poems, and a few other verses, some of uncertain authorship. His plays have been translated into every major living language and are performed more often than those of any other playwright.They also continue to be studied and reinterpreted. Shakespeare was born and raised in Stratford-upon-Avon, Warwickshire. At the age of 18, he married Anne Hathaway, with whom he had three children: Susanna and twins Hamnet and Judith. Sometime between 1585 and 1592, he began a successful career in London as an actor, writer, and part-owner of a playing company called the Lord Chamberlain's Men, later known as the King's Men. At age 49 (around 1613), he appears to have retired to Stratford, where he died three years later. Few records of Shakespeare's private life survive; this has stimulated considerable speculation about such matters as his physical appearance, his sexuality, his religious beliefs, and whether the works attributed to him were written by others.

Contents

All the world's a stage,

And all the men and women merely players;
They have their exits and their entrances,
And one man in his time plays many parts,
His acts being seven ages. At first, the infant,
Mewling and puking in the nurse's arms.
Then the whining schoolboy, with his satchel
And shining morning face, creeping like snail
Unwillingly to school. And then the lover,
Sighing like furnace, with a woeful ballad
Made to his mistress' eyebrow. Then a soldier,
Full of strange oaths and bearded like the pard,
Jealous in honor, sudden and quick in quarrel,
Seeking the bubble reputation
Even in the cannon's mouth. And then the justice,
In fair round belly with good capon lined,
With eyes severe and beard of formal cut,
Full of wise saws and modern instances;
And so he plays his part. The sixth age shifts
Into the lean and slippered pantaloon,
With spectacles on nose and pouch on side;
His youthful hose, well saved, a world too wide
For his shrunk shank, and his big manly voice,
Turning again toward childish treble, pipes
And whistles in his sound. Last scene of all,
That ends this strange eventful history,
Is second childishness and mere oblivion,
Sans teeth, sans eyes, sans taste, sans everything.

A Fairy Song

Over hill, over dale,
Thorough bush, thorough brier,
Over park, over pale,
Thorough flood, thorough fire!
I do wander everywhere,
Swifter than the moon's sphere;
And I serve the Fairy Queen,
To dew her orbs upon the green;
The cowslips tall her pensioners be;
In their gold coats spots you see;
Those be rubies, fairy favours;
In those freckles live their savours;
I must go seek some dewdrops here,
And hang a pearl in every cowslip's ear.

Shall I Compare Thee To A Summer's Day? (Sonnet 18)

Shall I compare thee to a summer's day?
Thou art more lovely and more temperate.
Rough winds do shake the darling buds of May,
And summer's lease hath all too short a date.
Sometime too hot the eye of heaven shines,
And often is his gold complexion dimmed;
And every fair from fair sometime declines,
By chance, or nature's changing course, untrimmed;
But thy eternal summer shall not fade,
Nor lose possession of that fair thou ow'st,
Nor shall death brag thou wand'rest in his shade,
When in eternal lines to Time thou grow'st.
So long as men can breathe, or eyes can see,
So long lives this, and this gives life to thee.

Fear No More

Fear no more the heat o' the sun;
Nor the furious winter's rages,
Thou thy worldly task hast done,
Home art gone, and ta'en thy wages;
Golden lads and girls all must,
As chimney sweepers come to dust.

Fear no more the frown of the great,
Thou art past the tyrant's stroke:
Care no more to clothe and eat;
To thee the reed is as the oak:
The sceptre, learning, physic, must
All follow this, and come to dust.

Fear no more the lightning-flash,
Nor the all-dread thunder-stone;
Fear not slander, censure rash;
Thou hast finished joy and moan;
All lovers young, all lovers must
Consign to thee, and come to dust.

No exorciser harm thee!
Nor no witchcraft charm thee!
Ghost unlaid forbear thee!
Nothing ill come near thee!
Quiet consummation have;
And renowned be thy grave!

Blow, Blow, Thou Winter Wind

Blow, blow, thou winter wind
Thou art not so unkind
As man's ingratitude;
Thy tooth is not so keen,
Because thou art not seen,
Although thy breath be rude.

Heigh-ho! sing, heigh-ho! unto the green holly:
Most freindship if feigning, most loving mere folly:
Then heigh-ho, the holly!
This life is most jolly.

Freeze, freeze thou bitter sky,
That does not bite so nigh
As benefits forgot:
Though thou the waters warp,
Thy sting is not so sharp
As a friend remembered not.
Heigh-ho! sing, heigh-ho! unto the green holly:
Most friendship is feigning, most loving mere folly:
Then heigh-ho, the holly!
This life is most jolly.

O Mistress Mine, Where Are You Roaming? (Twelfth Night, Act Ii, Scene Iii)

O mistress mine, where are you roaming?
O stay and hear! your true-love's coming
That can sing both high and low;
Trip no further, pretty sweeting,
Journey's end in lovers' meeting-
Every wise man's son doth know.

What is love? 'tis not hereafter;
Present mirth hath present laughter;
What's to come is still unsure:
In delay there lies no plenty,-
Then come kiss me, Sweet and twenty,
Youth's a stuff will not endure.

Sonnet 116: Let Me Not To The Marriage Of True Minds

Let me not to the marriage of true minds
Admit impediments. Love is not love
Which alters when it alteration finds,
Or bends with the remover to remove.
O no, it is an ever-fixèd mark
That looks on tempests and is never shaken;
It is the star to every wand'ring bark,
Whose worth's unknown, although his height be taken.
Love's not Time's fool, though rosy lips and cheeks
Within his bending sickle's compass come;
Love alters not with his brief hours and weeks,
But bears it out even to the edge of doom.
If this be error and upon me proved,
I never writ, nor no man ever loved.

Hark! Hark! The Lark

Hark! hark! the lark at heaven's gate sings,
And Phoebus 'gins arise,
His steeds to water at those springs
On chalic'd flowers that lies;
And winking Mary-buds begin
To ope their golden eyes;
With everything that pretty is,
My lady sweet, arise:
Arise, arise!

A Madrigal

Crabbed Age and Youth
Cannot live together:
Youth is full of pleasance,
Age is full of care;
Youth like summer morn,
Age like winter weather;
Youth like summer brave,
Age like winter bare:
Youth is full of sports,
Age's breath is short,
Youth is nimble, Age is lame:
Youth is hot and bold,
Age is weak and cold,
Youth is wild, and Age is tame:-
Age, I do abhor thee;
Youth, I do adore thee;
O! my Love, my Love is young!
Age, I do defy thee-
O sweet shepherd, hie thee,
For methinks thou stay'st too long.

Bridal Song

ROSES, their sharp spines being gone,
Not royal in their smells alone,
But in their hue;
Maiden pinks, of odour faint,
Daisies smell-less, yet most quaint,
And sweet thyme true;

Primrose, firstborn child of Ver;
Merry springtime's harbinger,
With her bells dim;
Oxlips in their cradles growing,
Marigolds on death-beds blowing,
Larks'-heels trim;

All dear Nature's children sweet
Lie 'fore bride and bridegroom's feet,
Blessing their sense!
Not an angel of the air,
Bird melodious or bird fair,
Be absent hence!

The crow, the slanderous cuckoo, nor
The boding raven, nor chough hoar,
Nor chattering pye,
May on our bride-house perch or sing,
Or with them any discord bring,
But from it fly!

Sonnet 138 : When My Love Swears That She Is Made Of Truth

When my love swears that she is made of truth
I do believe her, though I know she lies,
That she might think me some untutored youth,
Unlearnèd in the world's false subtleties.
Thus vainly thinking that she thinks me young,
Although she knows my days are past the best,
Simply I credit her false-speaking tongue;
On both sides thus is simple truth suppressed.
But wherefore says she not she is unjust?
And wherefore say not I that I am old?
O, love's best habit is in seeming trust,
And age in love, loves not to have years told.
Therefore I lie with her, and she with me,
And in our faults by lies we flattered be.

Full Fathom Five

Full fathom five thy father lies;
Of his bones are coral made;
Those are pearls that were his eyes:
Nothing of him that doth fade
But doth suffer a sea-change
Into something rich and strange.
Sea-nymphs hourly ring his knell:
Ding-dong.
Hark! now I hear them,--ding-dong, bell.

Fairy Land I

OVER hill, over dale,
Thorough bush, thorough brier,
Over park, over pale,
Thorough flood, thorough fire,
I do wander everywhere,
Swifter than the moone's sphere;
And I serve the fairy queen,
To dew her orbs upon the green:
The cowslips tall her pensioners be;
In their gold coats spots you see;
Those be rubies, fairy favours,
In those freckles live their savours:
I must go seek some dew-drops here,
And hang a pearl in every cowslip's ear.

Sonnet 18 : Shall I Compare Thee To A Summer's Day?

Shall I compare thee to a summer's day?
Thou art more lovely and more temperate.
Rough winds do shake the darling buds of May,
And summer's lease hath all too short a date.
Sometime too hot the eye of heaven shines,
And often is his gold complexion dimmed;
And every fair from fair sometime declines,
By chance, or nature's changing course untrimmed.
But thy eternal summer shall not fade
Nor lose possession of that fair thou ow'st;
Nor shall death brag thou wand'rest in his shade,
When in eternal lines to time thou grow'st,
So long as men can breathe or eyes can see,
So long lives this, and this gives life to thee.

Winter

When icicles hang by the wall
And Dick the shepherd blows his nail
And Tom bears logs into the hall,
And milk comes frozen home in pail,
When Blood is nipped and ways be foul,
Then nightly sings the staring owl,
Tu-who;
Tu-whit, tu-who: a merry note,
While greasy Joan doth keel the pot.

When all aloud the wind doth blow,
And coughing drowns the parson's saw,
And birds sit brooding in the snow,
And Marian's nose looks red and raw
When roasted crabs hiss in the bowl,
Then nightly sings the staring owl,
Tu-who;
Tu-whit, tu-who: a merry note,
While greasy Joan doth keel the pot.

Aubade

HARK! hark! the lark at heaven's gate sings,
And Phoebus 'gins arise,
His steeds to water at those springs
On chaliced flowers that lies;
And winking Mary-buds begin
To ope their golden eyes:
With everything that pretty bin,
My lady sweet, arise!
Arise, arise!

Dirge Of The Three Queens

URNS and odours bring away!
Vapours, sighs, darken the day!
Our dole more deadly looks than dying;
Balms and gums and heavy cheers,
Sacred vials fill'd with tears,
And clamours through the wild air flying!

Come, all sad and solemn shows,
That are quick-eyed Pleasure's foes!
We convent naught else but woes.

From Venus And Adonis

But, lo! from forth a copse that neighbours by,
A breeding jennet, lusty, young, and proud,
Adonis' trampling courser doth espy,
And forth she rushes, snorts and neighs aloud;
The strong-neck'd steed, being tied unto a tree,
Breaketh his rein, and to her straight goes he.

Imperiously he leaps, he neighs, he bounds,
And now his woven girths he breaks asunder;
The bearing earth with his hard hoof he wounds,
Whose hollow womb resounds like heaven's thunder;
The iron bit he crushes 'tween his teeth
Controlling what he was controlled with.

His ears up-prick'd; his braided hanging mane
Upon his compass'd crest now stand on end;
His nostrils drink the air, and forth again,
As from a furnace, vapours doth he send:
His eye, which scornfully glisters like fire,
Shows his hot courage and his high desire.

Sometime her trots, as if he told the steps,
With gentle majesty and modest pride;
Anon he rears upright, curvets and leaps,
As who should say, 'Lo! thus my strength is tried;
And this I do to captivate the eye
Of the fair breeder that is standing by.'

What recketh he his rider's angry stir,

His flattering 'Holla,' or his 'Stand, I say?'
What cares he now for curb of pricking spur?
For rich caparisons or trapping gay?
He sees his love, and nothing else he sees,
Nor nothing else with his proud sight agrees.

Look, when a painter would surpass the life,
In limning out a well-proportion'd steed,
His art with nature's workmanship at strife,
As if the dead the living should exceed;
So did this horse excel a common one,
In shape, in courage, colour, pace and bone

Round-hoof'd, short-jointed, fetlocks shag and long,
Broad breast, full eye, small head, and nostril wide,
High crest, short ears, straight legs and passing strong,
Thin mane, thick tail, broad buttock, tender hide:
Look, what a horse should have he did not lack,
Save a proud rider on so proud a back.

Sometimes he scuds far off, and there he stares;
Anon he starts at stirring of a feather;
To bid the wind a race he now prepares,
And whe'r he run or fly they know not whether;
For through his mane and tail the high wind sings,
Fanning the hairs, who wave like feather'd wings.

He looks upon his love, and neighs unto her;
She answers him as if she knew his mind;
Being proud, as females are, to see him woo her,
She puts on outward strangeness, seems unkind,
Spurns at his love and scorns the heat he feels,
Beating his kind embracements with her heels.

Then, like a melancholy malcontent,

He vails his tail that, like a falling plume
Cool shadow to his melting buttock lent:
He stamps, and bites the poor flies in his fume.
His love, perceiving how he is enrag'd,
Grew kinder, and his fury was assuag'd.

His testy master goeth about to take him;
When lo! the unback'd breeder, full of fear,
Jealous of catching, swiftly doth forsake him,
With her the horse, and left Adonis there.
As they were mad, unto the wood they hie them,
Out-stripping crows that strive to over-fly them.

I prophesy they death, my living sorrow,
If thou encounter with the boar to-morrow.

"But if thou needs wilt hunt, be rul'd by me;
Uncouple at the timorous flying hare,
Or at the fox which lives by subtlety,
Or at the roe which no encounter dare:
Pursue these fearful creatures o'er the downs,
And on they well-breath'd horse keep with they hounds.

"And when thou hast on food the purblind hare,
Mark the poor wretch, to overshoot his troubles
How he outruns with winds, and with what care
He cranks and crosses with a thousand doubles:
The many musits through the which he goes
Are like a labyrinth to amaze his foes.

"Sometime he runs among a flock of sheep,
To make the cunning hounds mistake their smell,
And sometime where earth-delving conies keep,
To stop the loud pursuers in their yell,

And sometime sorteth with a herd of deer;
Danger deviseth shifts; wit waits on fear:

"For there his smell with other being mingled,
The hot scent-snuffing hounds are driven to doubt,
Ceasing their clamorous cry till they have singled
With much ado the cold fault cleanly out;
Then do they spend their mouths: Echo replies,
As if another chase were in the skies.

"By this, poor Wat, far off upon a hill,
Stands on his hinder legs with listening ear,
To hearken if his foes pursue him still:
Anon their loud alarums he doth hear;
And now his grief may be compared well
To one sore sick that hears the passing-bell.

"Then shalt thou see the dew-bedabbled wretch
Turn, and return, indenting with the way;
Each envious briar his weary legs doth scratch,
Each shadow makes him stop, each murmur stay:
For misery is trodden on by many,
And being low never reliev'd by any.

"Lie quietly, and hear a little more;
Nay, do not struggle, for thou shalt not rise:
To make thee hate the hunting of the boar,
Unlike myself thou hear'st me moralize,
Applying this to that, and so to so;
For love can comment upon every woe."

Sonnet 130: My Mistress' Eyes Are Nothing Like The Sun

My mistress' eyes are nothing like the sun;
Coral is far more red than her lips' red;
If snow be white, why then her breasts are dun;
If hairs be wires, black wires grow on her head.
I have seen roses damasked, red and white,
But no such roses see I in her cheeks,
And in some perfumes is there more delight
Than in the breath that from my mistress reeks.
I love to hear her speak, yet well I know,
That music hath a far more pleasing sound.
I grant I never saw a goddess go;
My mistress when she walks treads on the ground.
And yet, by heaven, I think my love as rare
As any she belied with false compare.

Silvia

WHO is Silvia? What is she?
That all our swains commend her?
Holy, fair, and wise is she;
The heaven such grace did lend her,
That she might admired be.

Is she kind as she is fair?
For beauty lives with kindness:
Love doth to her eyes repair,
To help him of his blindness;
And, being help'd, inhabits there.

Then to Silvia let us sing,
That Silvia is excelling;
She excels each mortal thing
Upon the dull earth dwelling:
To her let us garlands bring.

Fairy Land Ii

YOU spotted snakes with double tongue,
  Thorny hedgehogs, be not seen;
Newts and blind-worms, do no wrong;
  Come not near our fairy queen.

Philomel, with melody,
  Sing in our sweet lullaby;
Lulla, lulla, lullaby; lulla, lulla, lullaby!
  Never harm,
  Nor spell nor charm,
Come our lovely lady nigh;
So, good night, with lullaby.

Weaving spiders, come not here;
Hence, you long-legg'd spinners, hence!
Beetles black, approach not near;
  Worm nor snail, do no offence.

Philomel, with melody,
  Sing in our sweet lullaby;
Lulla, lulla, lullaby; lulla, lulla, lullaby!
  Never harm,
  Nor spell nor charm,
Come our lovely lady nigh;
So, good night, with lullaby.

It Was A Lover And His Lass

IT was a lover and his lass,
With a hey, and a ho, and a hey nonino,
That o'er the green corn-field did pass,
In the spring time, the only pretty ring time,
When birds do sing, hey ding a ding, ding;
Sweet lovers love the spring.

Between the acres of the rye,
With a hey, and a ho, and a hey nonino,
These pretty country folks would lie,
In the spring time, the only pretty ring time,
When birds do sing, hey ding a ding, ding;
Sweet lovers love the spring.

This carol they began that hour,
With a hey, and a ho, and a hey nonino,
How that life was but a flower
In the spring time, the only pretty ring time,
When birds do sing, hey ding a ding, ding;
Sweet lovers love the spring.

And, therefore, take the present time
With a hey, and a ho, and a hey nonino,
For love is crown'd with the prime
In the spring time, the only pretty ring time,
When birds do sing, hey ding a ding, ding;
Sweet lovers love the spring.

The Quality Of Mercy

The quality of mercy is not strain'd.
It droppeth as the gentle rain from heaven
Upon the place beneath. It is twice blest:
It blesseth him that gives, and him that takes.
'Tis mightiest in the mightiest; it becomes
The throned monarch better than his crown.
His scepter shows the force of temporal power,
The attribute to awe and majesty,
Wherein doth sit the dread and fear of kings;
But mercy is above this sceptered sway;
It is enthroned in the heart of kings;
It is an attribute to God himself;
And earthly power doth then show likest God's
When mercy seasons justice.

Sigh No More

Sigh no more, ladies, sigh no more,
Men were deceivers ever;
One foot in sea, and one on shore,
To one thing constant never.
Then sigh not so,
But let them go,
And be you blith and bonny,
Converting all your sounds of woe
Into Hey nonny, nonny.

Sing no more ditties, sing no mo
Of dumps so dull and heavy;
The fraud of men was ever so,
Since summer first was leavy.
Then sigh not so,
But let them go,
And be you blith and bonny,
Converting all your sounds of woe
Into Hey nonny, nonny.

Sonnet 141 : In Faith, I Do Not Love Thee With Mine Eyes

In faith, I do not love thee with mine eyes,
For they in thee a thousand errors note;
But 'tis my heart that loves what they despise,
Who in despite of view is pleased to dote.
Nor are mine cars with thy tongue's tune delighted,
Nor tender feeling to base touches prone,
Nor taste, nor smell, desire to be invited
To any sensual feast with thee alone;
But my five wits, nor my five senses can
Dissuade one foolish heart from serving thee,
Who leaves unswayed the likeness of a man,
Thy proud heart's slave and vassal wretch to be.
Only my plague thus far I count my gain,
That she that makes me sin awards me pain.

To Be, Or Not To Be (Hamlet, Act Iii, Scene I)

To be, or not to be: that is the question:
Whether 'tis nobler in the mind to suffer
The slings and arrows of outrageous fortune,
Or to take arms against a sea of troubles,
And by opposing end them? To die: to sleep;
No more; and by a sleep to say we end
The heart-ache and the thousand natural shocks
That flesh is heir to, 'tis a consummation
Devoutly to be wish'd. To die, to sleep;
To sleep: perchance to dream: ay, there's the rub;
For in that sleep of death what dreams may come
When we have shuffled off this mortal coil,
Must give us pause: there's the respect
That makes calamity of so long life;
For who would bear the whips and scorns of time,
The oppressor's wrong, the proud man's contumely,
The pangs of despised love, the law's delay,
The insolence of office and the spurns
That patient merit of the unworthy takes,
When he himself might his quietus make
With a bare bodkin? who would fardels bear,
To grunt and sweat under a weary life,
But that the dread of something after death,
The undiscover'd country from whose bourn
No traveller returns, puzzles the will
And makes us rather bear those ills we have
Than fly to others that we know not of?

Thus conscience does make cowards of us all;
And thus the native hue of resolution
Is sicklied o'er with the pale cast of thought,
And enterprises of great pith and moment
With this regard their currents turn awry,
And lose the name of action. —Soft you now!
The fair Ophelia! Nymph, in thy orisons
Be all my sins remember'd.

Sonnet 128: How Oft, When Thou, My Music, Music Play'st

How oft, when thou, my music, music play'st,
Upon that blessèd wood whose motion sounds
With thy sweet fingers when thou gently sway'st
The wiry concord that mine ear confounds,
Do I envy those jacks that nimble leap
To kiss the tender inward of thy hand,
Whilst my poor lips, which should that harvest reap,
At the wood's boldness by thee blushing stand!
To be so tickled, they would change their state
And situation with those dancing chips
O'er whom thy fingers walk with gentle gait,
Making dead wood more blest than living lips.
Since saucy jacks so happy are in this,
Give them thy fingers, me thy lips to kiss.

Sonnet 142 : Love Is My Sin, And Thy Dear Virtue Hate

Love is my sin, and thy dear virtue hate,
Hate of my sin, grounded on sinful loving,
O, but with mine, compare thou thine own state,
And thou shalt find it merits not reproving,
Or if it do, not from those lips of thine
That have profaned their scarlet ornaments
And sealed false bonds of love as oft as mine,
Robbed others' beds' revenues of their rents.
Be it lawful I love thee as thou lov'st those
Whom thine eyes woo as mine importune thee.
Root pity in thy heart, that when it grows
Thy pity may deserve to pitied be.
If thou dost seek to have what thou dost hide,
By self-example mayst thou be denied!

Orpheus With His Lute Made Trees

Orpheus with his lute made trees,
And the mountain tops that freeze,
Bow themselves, when he did sing:
To his music plants and flowers
Ever sprung; as sun and showers
There had made a lasting spring.

Everything that heard him play,
Even the billows of the sea,
Hung their heads, and then lay by.
In sweet music is such art,
Killing care and grief of heart
Fall asleep, or hearing, die.

Sonnet 1: From Fairest Creatures We Desire Increase

From fairest creatures we desire increase,
That thereby beauty's rose might never die,
But as the riper should by time decease,
His tender heir might bear his memory;
But thou contracted to thine own bright eyes,
Feed'st thy light's flame with self-substantial fuel,
Making a famine where abundance lies,
Thyself thy foe, to thy sweet self too cruel.
Thou that art now the world's fresh ornament,
And only herald to the gaudy spring,
Within thine own bud buriest thy content,
And tender churl mak'st waste in niggarding.
Pity the world, or else this glutton be:
To eat the world's due, by the grave and thee.

Not Marble Nor The Guilded Monuments (Sonnet 55)

Not marble nor the gilded monuments
Of princes shall outlive this powerful rhyme;
But you shall shine more bright in these contents
Than unswept stone, besmear'd with sluttish time.
When wasteful war shall statues overturn,
And broils root out the work of masonry,
Nor Mars his sword nor war's quick fire shall burn
The living record of your memory.
'Gainst death and all-oblivious enmity
Shall you pace forth; your praise shall still find room,
Even in the eyes of all posterity
That wear this world out to the ending doom.
So, till the judgment that yourself arise,
You live in this, and dwell in lovers' eyes.

O Never Say That I Was False Of Heart

O never say that I was false of heart,
Though absence seem'd my flame to qualify:
As easy might I from myself depart
As from my soul, which in thy breast doth lie;

That is my home of love; if I have ranged,
Like him that travels, I return again,
Just to the time, not with the time exchanged,
So that myself bring water for my stain.

Never believe, though in my nature reign'd
All frailties that besiege all kinds of blood,
That it could so preposterously be stain'd
To leave for nothing all thy sum of good:

For nothing this wide universe I call,
Save thou, my rose: in it thou art my all.

Sonnet 30 : When To The Sessions Of Sweet Silent Thought

When to the sessions of sweet silent thought
I summon up remembrance of things past,
I sigh the lack of many a thing I sought,
And with old woes new wail my dear time's waste.
Then can I drown an eye, unused to flow,
For precious friends hid in death's dateless night,
And weep afresh love's long since cancelled woe,
And moan th' expense of many a vanished sight.
Then can I grieve at grievances foregone,
And heavily from woe to woe tell o'er
The sad account of fore-bemoanèd moan,
Which I new pay as if not paid before.
But if the while I think on thee, dear friend,
All losses are restored and sorrows end.

Sonnet 17: Who Will Believe My Verse In Time To Come

Who will believe my verse in time to come
If it were filled with your most high deserts?
Though yet heaven knows it is but as a tomb
Which hides your life, and shows not half your parts:
If I could write the beauty of your eyes,
And in fresh numbers number all your graces,
The age to come would say, "This poet lies,
Such heavenly touches ne'er touched earthly faces."
So should my papers, yellowed with their age,
Be scorned like old men of less truth than tongue,
And your true rights be termed a poet's rage,
And stretchèd metre of an antique song.
But were some child of yours alive that time,
You should live twice, in it and in my rhyme.

Spring And Winter

WHEN daisies pied and violets blue,
And lady-smocks all silver-white,
And cuckoo-buds of yellow hue
Do paint the meadows with delight,
The cuckoo then, on every tree,
Mocks married men; for thus sings he,
Cuckoo!
Cuckoo, cuckoo! - O word of fear,
Unpleasing to a married ear!

When shepherds pipe on oaten straws,
And merry larks are ploughmen's clocks,
When turtles tread, and rooks, and daws,
And maidens bleach their summer smocks
The cuckoo then, on every tree,
Mocks married men; for thus sings he,
Cuckoo!
Cuckoo, cuckoo! - O word of fear,
Unpleasing to a married ear!

Sonnet 23 : As An Unperfect Actor On The Stage

As an unperfect actor on the stage
Who with his fear is put beside his part,
Or some fierce thing replete with too much rage,
Whose strength's abundance weakens his own heart,
So I, for fear of trust, forget to say
The perfect ceremony of love's rite,
And in mine own love's strength seem to decay,
O'ercharged with burden of mine own love's might.
O, let my books be then the eloquence
And dumb presagers of my speaking breast,
Who plead for love, and look for recompense
More than that tongue that more hath more expressed.
O, learn to read what silent love hath writ,
To hear with eyes belongs to love's fine wit.

That Time Of Year Thou Mayst In Me Behold (Sonnet 73)

That time of year thou mayst in me behold
When yellow leaves, or none, or few, do hang
Upon those boughs which shake against the cold,
Bare ruined choirs, where late the sweet birds sang.
In me thou see'st the twilight of such day
As after sunset fadeth in the west;
Which by and by black night doth take away,
Death's second self, that seals all up in rest.
In me thou see'st the glowing of such fire,
That on the ashes of his youth doth lie,
As the deathbed whereon it must expire,
Consumed with that which it was nourished by.
This thou perceiv'st, which makes thy love more strong,
To love that well which thou must leave ere long.

Witches Chant (From Macbeth)

Round about the couldron go:
In the poisones entrails throw.
Toad,that under cold stone
Days and nights has thirty-one
Sweated venom sleeping got,
Boil thou first in the charmed pot.
Double,double toil and trouble;
Fire burn and cauldron bubble.

Fillet of a fenny snake,
In the cauldron boil and bake;
Eye of newt and toe of frog,
Wool of bat and tongue of dog,
Adder's fork and blindworm's sting,
Lizard's leg and howlet's wing.
For charm of powerful trouble,
Like a hell-broth boil and bubble.
Double,double toil and trouble;
Fire burn and couldron bubble.

Scale of dragon,tooth of wolf,
Witch's mummy, maw and gulf
Of the ravin'd salt-sea shark,
Root of hemlock digg'd in the dark,
Liver of blaspheming Jew;
Gall of goat; andslips of yew
silver'd in the moon's eclipse;
Nose of Turk, and Tartar's lips;
Finger of birth-strangled babe

Ditch-deliver'd by the drab,-
Make the gruel thick and slab:
Add thereto a tiger's chaudron,
For ingrediants of our cauldron.
Double,double toil and trouble,
Fire burn and cauldron bubble.

Sonnet 147: My Love Is As A Fever, Longing Still

My love is as a fever, longing still
For that which longer nurseth the disease,
Feeding on that which doth preserve the ill,
Th' uncertain sickly appetite to please.
My reason, the physician to my love,
Angry that his prescriptions are not kept,
Hath left me, and I desperate now approve
Desire is death, which physic did except.
Past cure I am, now reason is past care,
And frantic-mad with evermore unrest;
My thoughts and my discourse as mad men's are,
At random from the truth vainly expressed.
For I have sworn thee fair, and thought thee bright,
Who art as black as hell, as dark as night.

Sonnet 144: Two Loves I Have, Of Comfort And Despair

Two loves I have, of comfort and despair,
Which like two spirits do suggest me still:
The better angel is a man right fair,
The worser spirit a woman coloured ill.
To win me soon to hell, my female evil
Tempteth my better angel from my side,
And would corrupt my saint to be a devil,
Wooing his purity with her foul pride.
And whether that my angel be turned fiend,
Suspect I may, yet not directly tell;
But being both from me both to each friend,
I guess one angel in another's hell.
Yet this shall I ne'er know, but live in doubt,
Till my bad angel fire my good one out.

The Phoenix And The Turtle

Let the bird of loudest lay,
On the sole Arabian tree,
Herald sad and trumpet be,
To whose sound chaste wings obey.

But thou, shrieking harbinger,
Foul pre-currer of the fiend,
Augur of the fever's end,
To this troop come thou not near.

From this session interdict
Every fowl of tyrant wing,
Save the eagle, feather'd king:
Keep the obsequy so strict.

Let the priest in surplice white,
That defunctive music can,
Be the death-divining swan,
Lest the requiem lack his right.

And thou, treble-dated crow,
That thy sable gender mak'st
With the breath thou giv'st and tak'st,
'Mongst our mourners shalt thou go.

Here the anthem doth commence:
Love and constancy is dead;
Phoenix and the turtle fled
In a mutual flame from hence.

So they lov'd, as love in twain
Had the essence but in one;
Two distincts, division none:
Number there in love was slain.

Hearts remote, yet not asunder;
Distance, and no space was seen
'Twixt the turtle and his queen;
But in them it were a wonder.

So between them love did shine,
That the turtle saw his right
Flaming in the phoenix' sight:
Either was the other's mine.

Property was thus appall'd,
That the self was not the same;
Single nature's double name
Neither two nor one was call'd.

Reason, in itself confounded,
Saw division grow together;
To themselves yet either-neither,
Simple were so well compounded.

That it cried how true a twain
Seemeth this concordant one!
Love hath reason, reason none
If what parts can so remain.

Whereupon it made this threne
To the phoenix and the dove,
Co-supreme and stars of love;
As chorus to their tragic scene.

THRENOS.

Beauty, truth, and rarity.
Grace in all simplicity,
Here enclos'd in cinders lie.

Death is now the phoenix' nest;
And the turtle's loyal breast
To eternity doth rest,

Leaving no posterity:-
'Twas not their infirmity,
It was married chastity.

Truth may seem, but cannot be:
Beauty brag, but 'tis not she;
Truth and beauty buried be.

To this urn let those repair
That are either true or fair;
For these dead birds sigh a prayer.

Sonnets Xxix: When, In Disgrace With Fortune And Men's Eyes

When, in disgrace with fortune and men's eyes,
I all alone beweep my outcast state
And trouble deaf heaven with my bootless cries
And look upon myself and curse my fate,
Wishing me like to one more rich in hope,
Featur'd like him, like him with friends possess'd,
Desiring this man's art and that man's scope,
With what I most enjoy contented least;
Yet in these thoughts myself almost despising,
Haply I think on thee, and then my state,
Like to the lark at break of day arising
From sullen earth, sings hymns at heaven's gate;
For thy sweet love remember'd such wealth brings
That then I scorn to change my state with kings.

Sonnet 134: So, Now I Have Confessed That He Is Thine

So, now I have confessed that he is thine,
And I my self am mortgaged to thy will,
Myself I'll forfeit, so that other mine
Thou wilt restore to be my comfort still.
But thou wilt not, nor he will not be free,
For thou art covetous, and he is kind,
He learned but surety-like to write for me
Under that bond that him as fist doth bind.
The statute of thy beauty thou wilt take,
Thou usurer, that putt'st forth all to use,
And sue a friend, came debtor for my sake;
So him I lose through my unkind abuse.
Him have I lost, thou hast both him and me;
He pays the whole, and yet am I not free.

Sonnet 27: Weary With Toil, I Haste Me to My Bed

Weary with toil, I haste me to my bed,
The dear respose for limbs with travel tirèd;
But then begins a journey in my head
To work my mind, when body's work's expirèd.
For then my thoughts, from far where I abide,
Intend a zealous pilgrimage to thee,
And keep my drooping eyelids open wide,
Looking on darkness which the blind do see;
Save that my soul's imaginary sight
Presents thy shadow to my sightless view,
Which like a jewel, hung in ghastly night,
Makes black night beauteous, and her old face new.
Lo thus by day my limbs, by night my mind,
For thee and for myself no quiet find.

Sonnet 73: That Time Of Year Thou Mayst In Me Behold

That time of year thou mayst in me behold,
When yellow leaves, or none, or few do hang
Upon those boughs which shake against the cold,
Bare ruined choirs where late the sweet birds sang.
In me thou seest the twilight of such day
As after sunset fadeth in the west,
Which by and by black night doth take away,
Death's second self that seals up all in rest.
In me thou seest the glowing of such fire
That on the ashes of his youth doth lie
As the death-bed whereon it must expire,
Consumed with that which it was nourished by.
This thou perceiv'st, which makes thy love more strong,
To love that well which thou must leave ere long.

Sonnet 60: Like As The Waves Make Towards The Pebbled Shore

Like as the waves make towards the pebbled shore,
So do our minutes hasten to their end;
Each changing place with that which goes before,
In sequent toil all forwards do contend.
Nativity once in the main of light,
Crawls to maturity, wherewith being crowned,
Crookèd eclipses 'gainst his glory fight,
And Time that gave doth now his gift confound.
Time doth transfix the flourish set on youth,
And delves the parallels in beauty's brow,
Feeds on the rarities of nature's truth,
And nothing stands but for his scythe to mow.
And yet to times in hope my verse shall stand,
Praising thy worth despite his cruel hand.

Sonnet 8 : Music To Hear, Why Hear'st Thou Music Sadly?

Music to hear, why hear'st thou music sadly?
Sweets with sweets war not, joy delights in joy.
Why lov'st thou that which thou receiv'st not gladly,
Or else receiv'st with pleasure thine annoy?
If the true concord of well-tunèd sounds,
By unions married, do offend thine ear,
They do but sweetly chide thee, who confounds
In singleness the parts that thou shouldst bear.
Mark how one string, sweet husband to another,
Strikes each in each by mutual ordering,
Resembling sire and child and happy mother,
Who, all in one, one pleasing note do sing;
Whose speechless song being many, seeming one,
Sings this to thee: "Thou single wilt prove none."

Sonnet 19: Devouring Time Blunt Thou The Lion's Paws

Devouring Time blunt thou the lion's paws,
And make the earth devour her own sweet brood,
Pluck the keen teeth from the fierce tiger's jaws,
And burn the long-lived phoenix, in her blood,
Make glad and sorry seasons as thou fleet'st,
And do whate'er thou wilt swift-footed Time
To the wide world and all her fading sweets.
But I forbid thee one most heinous crime:
O carve not with thy hours my love's fair brow,
Nor draw no lines there with thine antique pen,
Him in thy course untainted do allow,
For beauty's pattern to succeeding men.
Yet do thy worst old Time: despite thy wrong,
My love shall in my verse ever live young.

Sonnet 152: In Loving Thee Thou Know'st I Am Forsworn

In loving thee thou know'st I am forsworn,
But thou art twice forsworn to me love swearing:
In act thy bed-vow broke and new faith torn
In vowing new hate after new love bearing.
But why of two oaths' breach do I accuse thee,
When I break twenty? I am perjured most,
For all my vows are oaths but to misuse thee,
And all my honest faith in thee is lost.
For I have sworn deep oaths of thy deep kindness,
Oaths of thy love, thy truth, thy constancy,
And to enlighten thee gave eyes to blindness,
Or made them swear against the thing they see.
For I have sworn thee fair. More perjured eye,
To swear against the truth so foul a lie!

Sonnet 1: From Fairest Creatures We Desire Increase

From fairest creatures we desire increase,
That thereby beauty's rose might never die,
But as the riper should by time decease,
His tender heir might bear his memory;
But thou contracted to thine own bright eyes,
Feed'st thy light's flame with self-substantial fuel,
Making a famine where abundance lies,
Thyself thy foe, to thy sweet self too cruel.
Thou that art now the world's fresh ornament,
And only herald to the gaudy spring,
Within thine own bud buriest thy content,
And tender churl mak'st waste in niggarding.
Pity the world, or else this glutton be:
To eat the world's due, by the grave and thee.

Sonnet 150: O From What Power Hast Thou This Powerful Might

O, from what power hast thou this powerful might
With insufficiency my heart to sway?
To make me give the lie to my true sight,
And swear that brightness doth not grace the day?
Whence hast thou this becoming of things ill,
That in the very refuse of thy deeds
There is such strength and warrantise of skill
That, in my mind, thy worst all best exceeds?
Who taught thee how to make me love thee more,
The more I hear and see just cause of hate?
O, though I love what others do abhor,
With others thou shouldst not abhor my state.
If thy unworthiness raised love in me,
More worthy I to be beloved of thee.

Sonnet 67: Ah, Wherefore With Infection Should He Live

Ah, wherefore with infection should he live,
And with his presence grace impiety,
That sin by him advantage should achieve,
And lace it self with his society?
Why should false painting imitate his cheek,
And steal dead seeming of his living hue?
Why should poor beauty indirectly seek
Roses of shadow, since his rose is true?
Why should he live, now Nature bankrupt is,
Beggared of blood to blush through lively veins,
For she hath no exchequer now but his,
And proud of many, lives upon his gains?
O, him she stores, to show what wealth she had
In days long since, before these last so bad.

Sonnet 149 : Canst Thou, O Cruel, Say I Love Thee Not

Canst thou, O cruel, say I love thee not,
When I against my self with thee partake?
Do I not think on thee when I forgot
Am of my self, all tyrant, for thy sake?
Who hateth thee that I do call my friend?
On whom frown'st thou that I do fawn upon?
Nay, if thou lour'st on me, do I not spend
Revenge upon my self with present moan?
What merit do I in my self respect,
That is so proud thy service to despise,
When all my best doth worship thy defect,
Commanded by the motion of thine eyes?
But, love, hate on, for now I know thy mind:
Those that can see thou lov'st, and I am blind.

Sonnet 15:

When I consider everything that grows
Holds in perfection but a little moment,
That this huge stage presenteth nought but shows
Whereon the stars in secret influence comment;
When I perceive that men as plants increase,
Cheered and check'd even by the selfsame sky,
Vaunt in their youthful sap, at height decrease,
And wear their brave state out of memory;
Then the conceit of this inconstant stay
Sets you most rich in youth before my sight,
Where wasteful Time debateth with Decay
To change your day of youth to sullied night;
And all in war with Time for love of you,
As he takes from you, I engraft you new.

Sonnet 129 : Th' Expense Of Spirit In A Waste Of Shame

Th' expense of spirit in a waste of shame
Is lust in action; and, till action, lust
Is perjured, murderous, bloody full of blame,
Savage, extreme, rude, cruel, not to trust,
Enjoyed no sooner but despisèd straight,
Past reason hunted, and no sooner had
Past reason hated as a swallowed bait
On purpose laid to make the taker mad.
Mad in pursuit, and in possession so;
Had, having, and in quest to have, extreme;
A bliss in proof, and proved, a very woe,
Before a joy proposed; behind, a dream.
All this the world well knows, yet none knows well
To shun the heaven that leads men to this hell

Sonnet 16: But Wherefore Do Not You A Mightier Way

But wherefore do not you a mightier way
Make war upon this bloody tyrant, Time,
And fortify your self in your decay
With means more blessèd than my barren rhyme?
Now stand you on the top of happy hours,
And many maiden gardens yet unset,
With virtuous wish would bear you living flowers,
Much liker than your painted counterfeit:
So should the lines of life that life repair
Which this, Time's pencil, or my pupil pen
Neither in inward worth nor outward fair
Can make you live your self in eyes of men.
To give away your self keeps your self still,
And you must live drawn by your own sweet skill.

Sonnet Xviii: Shall I Compare Thee To A Summer's Day

Shall I compare thee to a summer's day?
Thou art more lovely and more temperate:
Rough winds do shake the darling buds of May,
And summer's lease hath all too short a date:
Sometime too hot the eye of heaven shines,
And often is his gold complexion dimm'd;
And every fair from fair sometime declines,
By chance or nature's changing course untrimm'd;
But thy eternal summer shall not fade
Nor lose possession of that fair thou owest;
Nor shall Death brag thou wander'st in his shade,
When in eternal lines to time thou growest:
So long as men can breathe or eyes can see,
So long lives this and this gives life to thee.

Sonnet 136: If Thy Soul Check Thee That I Come So Near

If thy soul check thee that I come so near,
Swear to thy blind soul that I was thy Will,
And will thy soul knows is admitted there;
Thus far for love, my love suit, sweet, fulfil.
Will will fulfil the treasure of thy love,
Ay, fill it full with wills, and my will one.
In things of great receipt with case we prove
Among a number one is reckoned none.
Then in the number let me pass untold,
Though in thy store's account I one must be;
For nothing hold me, so it please thee hold
That nothing me, a something, sweet, to thee.
Make but my name thy love, and love that still,
And then thou lov'st me for my name is Will.

Sonnet 97: How Like A Winter Hath My Absence Been

How like a winter hath my absence been
From thee, the pleasure of the fleeting year!
What freezings have I felt, what dark days seen!
What old December's bareness everywhere!
And yet this time removed was summer's time,
The teeming autumn, big with rich increase,
Bearing the wanton burden of the prime,
Like widowed wombs after their lords' decease:
Yet this abundant issue seemed to me
But hope of orphans, and unfathered fruit,
For summer and his pleasures wait on thee,
And thou away, the very birds are mute.
Or, if they sing, 'tis with so dull a cheer,
That leaves look pale, dreading the winter's near.

Now, My Co-Mates And Brothers In Exile

Now, my co-mates and brothers in exile,
Hath not old customs make this life more sweet
Than that of painted pomp? Are not these woods
More free from peril than the envious court!
Here feel we not the penalty of Adam,
The seasons difference; as the icy fang
And churlish chiding of the winters wind,
Which when it bites and blows upon my body,
Even till I shrink with cold, I smile and say
This is no flattery; these are counsellors
That feelingly persuade me what I am.
Sweet are the uses of adversity;
Which, like the toad, ugly and venomous,
Wears yet a precious jewel in his head;
And this our life, exempt from public haunt,
Finds tongues in trees, books in the running brooks,
Sermons in stones, and good in everything.
I would not change it.

The Blossom

ON a day--alack the day!--
Love, whose month is ever May,
Spied a blossom passing fair
Playing in the wanton air:
Through the velvet leaves the wind
All unseen 'gan passage find;
That the lover, sick to death,
Wish'd himself the heaven's breath.
Air, quoth he, thy cheeks may blow;
Air, would I might triumph so!
But, alack, my hand is sworn
Ne'er to pluck thee from thy thorn:
Vow, alack, for youth unmeet;
Youth so apt to pluck a sweet!
Do not call it sin in me
That I am forsworn for thee;
Thou for whom e'en Jove would swear
Juno but an Ethiop were;
And deny himself for Jove,
Turning mortal for thy love.

Sonnet 126: O Thou, My Lovely Boy, Who In Thy Power

O thou, my lovely boy, who in thy power
Dost hold Time's fickle glass his fickle hour;
Who hast by waning grown, and therein show'st
Thy lovers withering, as thy sweet self grow'st.
If Nature, sovereign mistress over wrack,
As thou goest onwards, still will pluck thee back,
She keeps thee to this purpose, that her skill
May Time disgrace, and wretched minutes kill.
Yet fear her, O thou minion of her pleasure!
She may detain, but not still keep her treasure.
Her audit, though delayed, answered must be,
And her quietus is to render thee.

Sonnet 57: Being Your Slave, What Should I Do But Tend

Being your slave, what should I do but tend
Upon the hours and times of your desire?
I have no precious time at all to spend,
Nor services to do, till you require.
Nor dare I chide the world-without-end hour,
Whilst I, my sovereign, watch the clock for you,
Nor think the bitterness of absence sour
When you have bid your servant once adieu.
Nor dare I question with my jealous thought
Where you may be, or your affairs suppose,
But, like a sad slave, stay and think of naught
Save where you are, how happy you make those.
So true a fool is love that in your will,
Though you do any thing, he thinks no ill.

Sonnet 11: As Fast As Thou Shalt Wane, So Fast Thou Grow'st

As fast as thou shalt wane, so fast thou grow'st
In one of thine, from that which thou departest,
And that fresh blood which youngly thou bestow'st,
Thou mayst call thine when thou from youth convertest.
Herein lives wisdom, beauty, and increase;
Without this folly, age, and cold decay,
If all were minded so, the times should cease,
And threescore year would make the world away.
Let those whom Nature hath not made for store,
Harsh, featureless, and rude, barrenly perish;
Look whom she best endowed, she gave the more,
Which bounteous gift thou shouldst in bounty cherish.
She carved thee for her seal, and meant thereby,
Thou shouldst print more, not let that copy die.

Take, O Take Those Lips Away

TAKE, O take those lips away,
That so sweetly were forsworn;
And those eyes, the break of day,
Lights that do mislead the morn!
But my kisses bring again,
Bring again;
Seals of love, but seal'd in vain,
Seal'd in vain!

Sonnet 120: That You Were Once Unkind Befriends Me Now

That you were once unkind befriends me now,
And for that sorrow, which I then did feel,
Needs must I under my transgression bow,
Unless my nerves were brass or hammered steel.
For if you were by my unkindness shaken
As I by yours, y'have passed a hell of time,
And I, a tyrant, have no leisure taken
To weigh how once I suffered in your crime.
O, that our night of woe might have remembered
My deepest sense how hard true sorrow hits,
And soon to you, as you to me then, tendered
The humble salve which wounded bosoms fits!
But that your trespass now becomes a fee;
Mine ransoms yours, and yours must ransom me.

Sonnet 27: Weary With Toil, I Haste Me To My Bed

Weary with toil, I haste me to my bed,
The dear respose for limbs with travel tirèd;
But then begins a journey in my head
To work my mind, when body's work's expirèd.
For then my thoughts, from far where I abide,
Intend a zealous pilgrimage to thee,
And keep my drooping eyelids open wide,
Looking on darkness which the blind do see;
Save that my soul's imaginary sight
Presents thy shadow to my sightless view,
Which like a jewel, hung in ghastly night,
Makes black night beauteous, and her old face new.
Lo thus by day my limbs, by night my mind,
For thee and for myself no quiet find.

Sonnet 64: When I Have Seen By Time's Fell Hand Defaced

When I have seen by Time's fell hand defaced
The rich-proud cost of outworn buried age;
When sometime lofty towers I see down-razed
And brass eternal slave to mortal rage;
When I have seen the hungry ocean gain
Advantage on the kingdom of the shore,
And the firm soil win of the watery main,
Increasing store with loss, and loss with store;
When I have seen such interchange of state,
Or state it self confounded to decay,
Ruin hath taught me thus to ruminate
That Time will come and take my love away.
This thought is as a death which cannot choose
But weep to have that which it fears to lose.

Sonnet 126: O Thou, My Lovely Boy, Who In Thy Power

O thou, my lovely boy, who in thy power
Dost hold Time's fickle glass his fickle hour;
Who hast by waning grown, and therein show'st
Thy lovers withering, as thy sweet self grow'st.
If Nature, sovereign mistress over wrack,
As thou goest onwards, still will pluck thee back,
She keeps thee to this purpose, that her skill
May Time disgrace, and wretched minutes kill.
Yet fear her, O thou minion of her pleasure!
She may detain, but not still keep her treasure.
Her audit, though delayed, answered must be,
And her quietus is to render thee.

Sonnet 22: My Glass Shall Not Persuade Me I Am Old

My glass shall not persuade me I am old
So long as youth and thou are of one date;
But when in thee Time's furrows I behold,
Then look I death my days should expiate.
For all that beauty that doth cover thee
Is but the seemly raiment of my heart,
Which in thy breast doth live, as thine in me.
How can I then be elder than thou art?
O, therefore, love, be of thyself so wary
As I not for myself, but for thee will,
Bearing thy heart, which I will keep so chary
As tender nurse her babe from faring ill.
Presume not on thy heart when mine is slain;
Thou gav'st me thine, not to give back again.

Sonnet 35: No More Be Grieved At That Which Thou Hast Done

No more be grieved at that which thou hast done.
Roses have thorns, and silver fountains mud,
Clouds and eclipses stain both moon and sun,
And loathsome canker lives in sweetest bud.
All men make faults, and even I in this,
Authorizing thy trespass with compare,
Myself corrupting, salving thy amiss,
Excusing thy sins more than thy sins are.
For to thy sensual fault I bring in sense—
Thy adverse party is thy advocate—
And 'gainst my self a lawful plea commence.
Such civil war is in my love and hate
That I an accessary needs must be
To that sweet thief which sourly robs from me.

Sonnet 139: O, Call Not Me To Justify The Wrong

O, call not me to justify the wrong
That thy unkindness lays upon my heart
Wound me not with thine eye but with thy tongue;
Use power with power, and slay me not by art.
Tell me thou lov'st elsewhere, but in my sight,
Dear heart forbear to glance thine eye aside;
What need'st thou wound with cunning when thy might
Is more than my o'erpressed defence can bide?
Let me excuse thee: "Ah, my love well knows,
Her pretty looks have been mine enemies,
And therefore from my face she turns my foes,
That they elsewhere might dart their injuries."
Yet do not so; but since I am near slain,
Kill me outright with looks and rid my pain.

Sonnet 58 : That God Forbid, That Made Me First Your Slave

That god forbid, that made me first your slave,
I should in thought control your times of pleasure,
Or at your hand th' account of hours to crave,
Being your vassal bound to stay your leisure!
O, let me suffer, being at your beck,
Th' imprisoned absence of your liberty,
And patience tame to sufferance, bide each check,
Without accusing you of injury.
Be where you list, your charter is so strong
That you your self may privilage your time
To what you will; to you it doth belong
Your self to pardon of self-doing crime.
I am to wait, though waiting so be hell,
Not blame your pleasure, be it ill or well.

Sonnet Cii

My love is strengthen'd, though more weak in seeming;
I love not less, though less the show appear:
That love is merchandized whose rich esteeming
The owner's tongue doth publish every where.
Our love was new and then but in the spring
When I was wont to greet it with my lays,
As Philomel in summer's front doth sing
And stops her pipe in growth of riper days:
Not that the summer is less pleasant now
Than when her mournful hymns did hush the night,
But that wild music burthens every bough
And sweets grown common lose their dear delight.
Therefore like her I sometime hold my tongue,
Because I would not dull you with my song.

Sonnet 99: The Forward Violet Thus Did I Chide

The forward violet thus did I chide:
"Sweet thief, whence didst thou steal thy sweet that smells,
If not from my love's breath? The purple pride
Which on thy soft check for complexion dwells
In my love's veins thou hast too grossly dyed."
The lily I condemnèd for thy hand,
And buds of marjoram had stol'n thy hair;
The roses fearfully on thorns did stand,
One blushing shame, another white despair;
A third, nor red, nor white, had stol'n of both,
And to his robbery had annexed thy breath,
But, for his theft, in pride of all his growth
A vengeful canker eat him up to death.
More flowers I noted, yet I none could see,
But sweet or colour it had stol'n from thee.

Sonnet 78: So Oft Have I Invoked Thee For My Muse

So oft have I invoked thee for my Muse,
And found such fair assistance in my verse
As every alien pen hath got my use,
And under thee their poesy disperse.
Thine eyes, that taught the dumb on high to sing,
And heavy ignorance aloft to fly,
Have added feathers to the learnèd's wing
And given grace a double majesty.
Yet be most proud of that which I compile,
Whose influence is thine, and born of thee.
In others' works thou dost but mend the style,
And arts with thy sweet graces gracèd be.
But thou art all my art, and dost advance
As high as learning my rude ignorance.

Sonnet 4: Unthrifty Loveliness, Why Dost Thou Spend

Unthrifty loveliness, why dost thou spend
Upon thy self thy beauty's legacy?
Nature's bequest gives nothing, but doth lend,
And being frank she lends to those are free.
Then, beauteous niggard why dost thou abuse,
The bounteous largess given thee to give?
Profitless usurer, why dost thou use
So great a sum of sums yet canst not live?
For having traffic with thyself alone,
Thou of thyself thy sweet self dost deceive.
Then how when nature calls thee to be gone,
What acceptable audit canst thou leave?
Thy unused beauty must be tombed with thee,
Which usèd, lives th' executor to be.

Sonnet Cxvi

Let me not to the marriage of true minds
Admit impediments. Love is not love
Which alters when it alteration finds,
Or bends with the remover to remove:
O no! it is an ever-fixed mark
That looks on tempests and is never shaken;
It is the star to every wandering bark,
Whose worth's unknown, although his height be taken.
Love's not Time's fool, though rosy lips and cheeks
Within his bending sickle's compass come:
Love alters not with his brief hours and weeks,
But bears it out even to the edge of doom.
If this be error and upon me proved,
I never writ, nor no man ever loved.

Sonnet 48: How Careful Was I, When I Took My Way

How careful was I, when I took my way,
Each trifle under truest bars to thrust,
That to my use it might unusèd stay
From hands of falsehood, in sure wards of trust!
But thou, to whom my jewels trifles are,
Most worthy comfort, now my greatest grief,
Thou best of dearest, and mine only care,
Art left the prey of every vulgar thief.
Thee have I not locked up in any chest,
Save where thou art not—though I feel thou art—
Within the gentle closure of my breast,
From whence at pleasure thou mayst come and part;
And even thence thou wilt be stol'n, I fear,
For truth proves thievish for a prize so dear.

Sonnet Cxlv

Those lips that Love's own hand did make
Breathed forth the sound that said 'I hate'
To me that languish'd for her sake;
But when she saw my woeful state,
Straight in her heart did mercy come,
Chiding that tongue that ever sweet
Was used in giving gentle doom,
And taught it thus anew to greet:
'I hate' she alter'd with an end,
That follow'd it as gentle day
Doth follow night, who like a fiend
From heaven to hell is flown away;
'I hate' from hate away she threw,
And saved my life, saying 'not you.'

Sonnet 37: As A Decrepit Father Takes Delight

As a decrepit father takes delight
To see his active child do deeds of youth,
So I, made lame by Fortune's dearest spite,
Take all my comfort of thy worth and truth.
For whether beauty, birth, or wealth, or wit,
Or any of these all, or all, or more,
Entitled in thy parts, do crownèd sit,
I make my love engrafted to this store.
So then I am not lame, poor, nor despised,
Whilst that this shadow doth such substance give
That I in thy abundance am sufficed
And by a part of all thy glory live.
Look what is best, that best I wish in thee.
This wish I have; then ten times happy me!

Sonnet Cv

Let not my love be call'd idolatry,
Nor my beloved as an idol show,
Since all alike my songs and praises be
To one, of one, still such, and ever so.
Kind is my love to-day, to-morrow kind,
Still constant in a wondrous excellence;
Therefore my verse to constancy confined,
One thing expressing, leaves out difference.
'Fair, kind and true' is all my argument,
'Fair, kind, and true' varying to other words;
And in this change is my invention spent,
Three themes in one, which wondrous scope affords.
'Fair, kind, and true,' have often lived alone,
Which three till now never kept seat in one.

Sonnet 86: Was It The Proud Full Sail Of His Great Verse

Was it the proud full sail of his great verse,
Bound for the prize of all-too-precious you,
That did my ripe thoughts in my brain inhearse,
Making their tomb the womb wherein they grew?
Was it his spirit, by spirits taught to write
Above a mortal pitch, that struck me dead?
No, neither he, nor his compeers by night
Giving him aid, my verse astonishèd.
He nor that affable familiar ghost
Which nightly gulls him with intelligence,
As victors of my silence cannot boast;
I was not sick of any fear from thence.
But when your countenance filled up his line,
Then lacked I matter, that enfeebled mine.

Sonnet Cviii

What's in the brain that ink may character
Which hath not figured to thee my true spirit?
What's new to speak, what new to register,
That may express my love or thy dear merit?
Nothing, sweet boy; but yet, like prayers divine,
I must, each day say o'er the very same,
Counting no old thing old, thou mine, I thine,
Even as when first I hallow'd thy fair name.
So that eternal love in love's fresh case
Weighs not the dust and injury of age,
Nor gives to necessary wrinkles place,
But makes antiquity for aye his page,
Finding the first conceit of love there bred
Where time and outward form would show it dead.

Sonnet Cvii: Not Mine Own Fears, Nor The Prophetic Soul

Not mine own fears, nor the prophetic soul
Of the wide world dreaming on things to come,
Can yet the lease of my true love control,
Suppos'd as forfeit to a confin'd doom.
The mortal moon hath her eclipse endur'd
And the sad augurs mock their own presage;
Incertainties now crown themselves assur'd
And peace proclaims olives of endless age.
Now with the drops of this most balmy time
My love looks fresh, and Death to me subscribes,
Since, spite of him, I'll live in this poor rhyme,
While he insults o'er dull and speechless tribes;
And thou in this shalt find thy monument,
When tyrants' crests and tombs of brass are spent.

Sonnet Cix

O, never say that I was false of heart,
Though absence seem'd my flame to qualify.
As easy might I from myself depart
As from my soul, which in thy breast doth lie:
That is my home of love: if I have ranged,
Like him that travels I return again,
Just to the time, not with the time exchanged,
So that myself bring water for my stain.
Never believe, though in my nature reign'd
All frailties that besiege all kinds of blood,
That it could so preposterously be stain'd,
To leave for nothing all thy sum of good;
For nothing this wide universe I call,
Save thou, my rose; in it thou art my all.
Now The Hungry Lion Roars
From "A Midsummer-Night's Dream," Act V. Scene 2

PUCK sings:

NOW the hungry lion roars,
And the wolf behowls the moon;
Whilst the heavy ploughman snores,
All with weary task fordone.
Now the wasted brands do glow,
Whilst the screech-owl, screeching loud,
Puts the wretch that lies in woe
In remembrance of a shroud.
Now it is the time of night,
That the graves, all gaping wide,
Every one lets forth his sprite,
In the churchway paths to glide:
And we fairies, that do run
By the triple Hecate's team,
From the presence of the sun,
Following darkness like a dream,
Now are frolic; not a mouse
Shall disturb this hallowed house:
I am sent with broom before
To sweep the dust behind the door.

Sonnet 135: Whoever Hath Her Wish, Thou Hast Thy Will

Whoever hath her wish, thou hast thy will,
And Will to boot, and Will in overplus;
More than enough am I that vex thee still,
To thy sweet will making addition thus.
Wilt thou, whose will is large and spacious,
Not once vouchsafe to hide my will in thine?
Shall will in others seem right gracious,
And in my will no fair acceptance shine?
The sea, all water, yet receives rain still,
And in abundance addeth to his store;
So thou being rich in will add to thy will
One will of mine to make thy large will more.
Let no unkind, no fair beseechers kill,
Think all but one, and me in that one Will.

Sonnet 54: O, How Much More Doth Beauty Beauteous Seem

O, how much more doth beauty beauteous seem
By that sweet ornament which truth doth give!
The rose looks fair, but fairer we it deem
For that sweet odour which doth in it live.
The canker blooms have full as deep a dye
As the perfumèd tincture of the roses,
Hang on such thorns, and play as wantonly
When summer's breath their maskèd buds discloses;
But, for their virtue only is their show,
They live unwooed and unrespected fade,
Die to themselves. Sweet roses do not so;
Of their sweet deaths are sweetest odours made.
And so of you, beauteous and lovely youth,
When that shall vade, by verse distills your truth.

Sonnet 84: Who Is It That Says Most, Which Can Say More

Who is it that says most, which can say more,
Than this rich praise -- that you alone are you,
In whose confine immurèd is the store
Which should example where your equal grew?
Lean penury within that pen doth dwell
That to his subject lends not some small glory;
But he that writes of you, if he can tell
That you are you, so dignifies his story.
Let him but copy what in you is writ,
Not making worse what nature made so clear,
And such a counterpart shall fame his wit,
Making his style admirèd everywhere.
You to your beauteous blessings add a curse,
Being fond on praise, which makes your praises worse.

Sonnet 107:

Not mine own fears, nor the prophetic soul
Of the wide world dreaming on things to come,
Can yet the lease of my true love control,
Suppos'd as forfeit to a confin'd doom.
The mortal moon hath her eclipse endur'd
And the sad augurs mock their own presage;
Incertainties now crown themselves assur'd
And peace proclaims olives of endless age.
Now with the drops of this most balmy time
My love looks fresh, and Death to me subscribes,
Since, spite of him, I'll live in this poor rhyme,
While he insults o'er dull and speechless tribes;
And thou in this shalt find thy monument,
When tyrants' crests and tombs of brass are spent.

Sonnet 85: My Tongue-Tied Muse In Manners Holds Her Still

My tongue-tied Muse in manners holds her still,
While comments of your praise, richly compiled,
Reserve their character with golden quill,
And precious phrase by all the Muses filed.
I think good thoughts, whilst other write good words,
And like unlettered clerk still cry "Amen"
To every hymn that able spirit affords
In polished form of well-refinèd pen.
Hearing you praised, I say "'Tis so, 'tis true,"
And to the most of praise add something more;
But that is in my thought, whose love to you,
Though words come hindmost, holds his rank before.
Then others for the breath of words respect,
Me for my dumb thoughts, speaking in effect.

Sonnet 15:

When I consider everything that grows
Holds in perfection but a little moment,
That this huge stage presenteth nought but shows
Whereon the stars in secret influence comment;
When I perceive that men as plants increase,
Cheered and check'd even by the selfsame sky,
Vaunt in their youthful sap, at height decrease,
And wear their brave state out of memory;
Then the conceit of this inconstant stay
Sets you most rich in youth before my sight,
Where wasteful Time debateth with Decay
To change your day of youth to sullied night;
And all in war with Time for love of you,
As he takes from you, I engraft you new.

Sonnet Ciii

Alack, what poverty my Muse brings forth,
That having such a scope to show her pride,
The argument all bare is of more worth
Than when it hath my added praise beside!
O, blame me not, if I no more can write!
Look in your glass, and there appears a face
That over-goes my blunt invention quite,
Dulling my lines and doing me disgrace.
Were it not sinful then, striving to mend,
To mar the subject that before was well?
For to no other pass my verses tend
Than of your graces and your gifts to tell;
And more, much more, than in my verse can sit
Your own glass shows you when you look in it.

Sonnet 81: Or I Shall Live Your Epitaph To Make

Or I shall live your epitaph to make,
Or you survive when I in earth am rotten,
From hence your memory death cannot take,
Although in me each part will be forgotten.
Your name from hence immortal life shall have,
Though I, once gone, to all the world must die;
The earth can yield me but a common grave,
When you entombèd in men's eyes shall lie.
Your monument shall be my gentle verse,
Which eyes not yet created shall o'er-read,
And tongues to be your being shall rehearse
When all the breathers of this world are dead.
You still shall live—such virtue hath my pen—
Where breath most breathes, even in the mouths of men.

Sonnet 62: Sin Of Self-Love Possesseth All Mine Eye

Sin of self-love possesseth all mine eye,
And all my soul, and all my every part;
And for this sin there is no remedy,
It is so grounded inward in my heart.
Methinks no face so gracious is as mine,
No shape so true, no truth of such account;
And for my self mine own worth do define,
As I all other in all worths surmount.
But when my glass shows me myself indeed
Beated and chapped with tanned antiquity,
Mine own self-love quite contrary I read;
Self so self-loving were iniquity.
'Tis thee, myself, that for my self I praise,
Painting my age with beauty of thy days.

Sonnet 6: Then Let Not Winter's Ragged Hand Deface

Then let not winter's ragged hand deface
In thee thy summer ere thou be distilled.
Make sweet some vial; treasure thou some place
With beauty's treasure ere it be self-killed.
That use is not forbidden usury
Which happies those that pay the willing loan;
That's for thyself to breed another thee,
Or ten times happier, be it ten for one,
Ten times thy self were happier than thou art,
If ten of thine ten times refigured thee;
Then what could death do, if thou shouldst depart,
Leaving thee living in posterity?
Be not self-willed, for thou art much too fair
To be death's conquest and make worms thine heir.

Sonnet Cxlii

Love is my sin and thy dear virtue hate,
Hate of my sin, grounded on sinful loving:
O, but with mine compare thou thine own state,
And thou shalt find it merits not reproving;
Or, if it do, not from those lips of thine,
That have profaned their scarlet ornaments
And seal'd false bonds of love as oft as mine,
Robb'd others' beds' revenues of their rents.
Be it lawful I love thee, as thou lovest those
Whom thine eyes woo as mine importune thee:
Root pity in thy heart, that when it grows
Thy pity may deserve to pitied be.
If thou dost seek to have what thou dost hide,
By self-example mayst thou be denied!

St. Crispin's Day Speech: From Henry V

WESTMORELAND. O that we now had here
But one ten thousand of those men in England
That do no work to-day!
KING. What's he that wishes so?
My cousin Westmoreland? No, my fair cousin;
If we are mark'd to die, we are enow
To do our country loss; and if to live,
The fewer men, the greater share of honour.
God's will! I pray thee, wish not one man more.
By Jove, I am not covetous for gold,
Nor care I who doth feed upon my cost;
It yearns me not if men my garments wear;
Such outward things dwell not in my desires.
But if it be a sin to covet honour,
I am the most offending soul alive.
No, faith, my coz, wish not a man from England.
God's peace! I would not lose so great an honour
As one man more methinks would share from me
For the best hope I have. O, do not wish one more!
Rather proclaim it, Westmoreland, through my host,
That he which hath no stomach to this fight,
Let him depart; his passport shall be made,
And crowns for convoy put into his purse;
We would not die in that man's company
That fears his fellowship to die with us.
This day is call'd the feast of Crispian.
He that outlives this day, and comes safe home,
Will stand a tip-toe when this day is nam'd,
And rouse him at the name of Crispian.

He that shall live this day, and see old age,
Will yearly on the vigil feast his neighbours,
And say "To-morrow is Saint Crispian."
Then will he strip his sleeve and show his scars,
And say "These wounds I had on Crispian's day."
Old men forget; yet all shall be forgot,
But he'll remember, with advantages,
What feats he did that day. Then shall our names,
Familiar in his mouth as household words-
Harry the King, Bedford and Exeter,
Warwick and Talbot, Salisbury and Gloucester-
Be in their flowing cups freshly rememb'red.
This story shall the good man teach his son;
And Crispin Crispian shall ne'er go by,
From this day to the ending of the world,
But we in it shall be remembered-
We few, we happy few, we band of brothers;
For he to-day that sheds his blood with me
Shall be my brother; be he ne'er so vile,
This day shall gentle his condition;
And gentlemen in England now-a-bed
Shall think themselves accurs'd they were not here,
And hold their manhoods cheap whiles any speaks
That fought with us upon Saint Crispin's day.

Sonnet 146:

Poor soul, the centre of my sinful earth,
[……] these rebel powers that thee array,
Why dost thou pine within and suffer dearth,
Painting thy outward walls so costly gay?
Why so large cost, having so short a lease,
Dost thou upon thy fading mansion spend?
Shall worms, inheritors of this excess,
Eat up thy charge? Is this thy body's end?
Then soul, live thou upon thy servant's loss
And let that pine to aggravate thy store;
Buy terms divine in selling hours of dross;
Within be fed, without be rich no more.
So shalt thou feed on Death, that feeds on men,
And, Death once dead, there's no more dying then.

Sonnet Cxi: O, For My Sake Do You With Fortune Chide

O, for my sake do you with Fortune chide,
The guilty goddess of my harmful deeds,
That did not better for my life provide
Than public means which public manners breeds.
Thence comes it that my name receives a brand,
And almost thence my nature is subdu'd
To what it works in, like the dyer's hand.
Pity me then and wish I were renew'd;
Whilst, like a willing patient, I will drink
Potions of eisel 'gainst my strong infection;
No bitterness that I will bitter think,
Nor double penance, to correct correction.
Pity me then, dear friend, and I assure ye
Even that your pity is enough to cure me.

Sonnets Xii

HOW like a Winter hath my absence been
From thee, the pleasure of the fleeting year!
What freezings have I felt, what dark days seen,
What old December's bareness everywhere!
And yet this time removed was summer's time;
The teeming Autumn, big with rich increase,
Bearing the wanton burden of the prime
Like widow'd wombs after their Lord's decease:
Yet this abundant issue seem'd to me
But hope of orphans and unfather'd fruit;
For Summer and his pleasures wait on thee,
And, thou away, the very birds are mute:
Or if they sing, 'tis with so dull a cheer
That leaves look pale, dreading the Winter 's near.

Sonnet 59: If There Be Nothing New, But That Which Is

If there be nothing new, but that which is
Hath been before, how are our brains beguiled,
Which, labouring for invention bear amis
The second burthen of a former child!
O, that record could with a backward look,
Even of five hundred courses of the sun,
Show me your image in some antique book,
Since mind at first in character was done.
That I might see what the old world could say
To this composèd wonder of your frame;
Whether we are mended, or whe'er better they,
Or whether revolution be the same.
O, sure I am the wits of former days
To subjects worse have given admiring praise.

Sonnet 67: Ah, Wherefore With Infection Should He Live

Ah, wherefore with infection should he live,
And with his presence grace impiety,
That sin by him advantage should achieve,
And lace it self with his society?
Why should false painting imitate his cheek,
And steal dead seeming of his living hue?
Why should poor beauty indirectly seek
Roses of shadow, since his rose is true?
Why should he live, now Nature bankrupt is,
Beggared of blood to blush through lively veins,
For she hath no exchequer now but his,
And proud of many, lives upon his gains?
O, him she stores, to show what wealth she had
In days long since, before these last so bad.

Sonnet Clii

In loving thee thou know'st I am forsworn,
But thou art twice forsworn, to me love swearing,
In act thy bed-vow broke and new faith torn,
In vowing new hate after new love bearing.
But why of two oaths' breach do I accuse thee,
When I break twenty? I am perjured most;
For all my vows are oaths but to misuse thee
And all my honest faith in thee is lost,
For I have sworn deep oaths of thy deep kindness,
Oaths of thy love, thy truth, thy constancy,
And, to enlighten thee, gave eyes to blindness,
Or made them swear against the thing they see;
For I have sworn thee fair; more perjured I,
To swear against the truth so foul a lie!

Macbeth, Act IV, Scene I

Three witches, casting a spell ...

Round about the cauldron go;
In the poison'd entrails throw.
Toad, that under cold stone
Days and nights hast thirty one
Swelter'd venom sleeping got,
Boil thou first i' the charmed pot.

Double, double toil and trouble;
Fire burn and cauldron bubble.

Fillet of a fenny snake,
In the cauldron boil and bake;
Eye of newt, and toe of frog,
Wool of bat, and tongue of dog,
Adder's fork, and blind-worm's sting,
Lizard's leg, and howlet's wing,
For a charm of powerful trouble,
Like a hell-broth boil and bubble.

Double, double toil and trouble;
Fire burn and cauldron bubble.

Sonnets Xxx : When To The Sessions Of Sweet Silent Thought

When to the sessions of sweet silent thought
I summon up remembrance of things past,
I sigh the lack of many a thing I sought,
And with old woes new wail my dear time's waste:
Then can I drown an eye, unus'd to flow,
For precious friends hid in death's dateless night,
And weep afresh love's long since cancell'd woe,
And moan th' expense of many a vanish'd sight;
Then can I grieve at grievances foregone,
And heavily from woe to woe tell o'er
The sad account of fore-bemoaned moan,
Which I new pay as if not paid before.
But if the while I think on thee, dear friend,
All losses are restor'd, and sorrows end.

Sonnet Cxlii

Love is my sin and thy dear virtue hate,
Hate of my sin, grounded on sinful loving:
O, but with mine compare thou thine own state,
And thou shalt find it merits not reproving;
Or, if it do, not from those lips of thine,
That have profaned their scarlet ornaments
And seal'd false bonds of love as oft as mine,
Robb'd others' beds' revenues of their rents.
Be it lawful I love thee, as thou lovest those
Whom thine eyes woo as mine importune thee:
Root pity in thy heart, that when it grows
Thy pity may deserve to pitied be.
If thou dost seek to have what thou dost hide,
By self-example mayst thou be denied!

Sonnet Lii

So am I as the rich, whose blessed key
Can bring him to his sweet up-locked treasure,
The which he will not every hour survey,
For blunting the fine point of seldom pleasure.
Therefore are feasts so solemn and so rare,
Since, seldom coming, in the long year set,
Like stones of worth they thinly placed are,
Or captain jewels in the carcanet.
So is the time that keeps you as my chest,
Or as the wardrobe which the robe doth hide,
To make some special instant special blest,
By new unfolding his imprison'd pride.
Blessed are you, whose worthiness gives scope,
Being had, to triumph, being lack'd, to hope.

Sonnet Civ

To me, fair friend, you never can be old,
For as you were when first your eye I eyed,
Such seems your beauty still. Three winters cold
Have from the forests shook three summers' pride,
Three beauteous springs to yellow autumn turn'd
In process of the seasons have I seen,
Three April perfumes in three hot Junes burn'd,
Since first I saw you fresh, which yet are green.
Ah! yet doth beauty, like a dial-hand,
Steal from his figure and no pace perceived;
So your sweet hue, which methinks still doth stand,
Hath motion and mine eye may be deceived:
For fear of which, hear this, thou age unbred;
Ere you were born was beauty's summer dead.

Sonnet Cxx

That you were once unkind befriends me now,
And for that sorrow which I then did feel
Needs must I under my transgression bow,
Unless my nerves were brass or hammer'd steel.
For if you were by my unkindness shaken
As I by yours, you've pass'd a hell of time,
And I, a tyrant, have no leisure taken
To weigh how once I suffered in your crime.
O, that our night of woe might have remember'd
My deepest sense, how hard true sorrow hits,
And soon to you, as you to me, then tender'd
The humble slave which wounded bosoms fits!
But that your trespass now becomes a fee;
Mine ransoms yours, and yours must ransom me.

Sonnet 72: O, Lest The World Should Task You To Recite

O, lest the world should task you to recite
What merit lived in me that you should love
After my death, dear love, forget me quite;
For you in me can nothing worthy prove—
Unless you would devise some virtuous lie
To do more for me than mine own desert,
And hang more praise upon deceasèd I
Than niggard truth would willingly impart.
O, lest your true love may seem false in this,
That you for love speak well of me untrue,
My name be buried where my body is,
And live no more to shame nor me nor you.
For I am shamed by that which I bring forth,
And so should you, to love things nothing worth.

The Dark Lady Sonnets (127 – 154)

And beauty slandered with a bastard shame:
For since each hand hath put on Nature's power,
Fairing the foul with Art's false borrowed face,
Sweet beauty hath no name, no holy bower,
But is profaned, if not lives in disgrace.
Therefore my mistress' eyes are raven black,
Her eyes so suited, and they mourners seem
At such who, not born fair, no beauty lack,
Sland'ring creation with a false esteem:
Yet so they mourn becoming of their woe,
That every tongue says beauty should look so.

CXXVIII

How oft when thou, my music, music play'st,
Upon that blessed wood whose motion sounds
With thy sweet fingers when thou gently sway'st
The wiry concord that mine ear confounds,
Do I envy those jacks that nimble leap,
To kiss the tender inward of thy hand,
Whilst my poor lips which should that harvest reap,
At the wood's boldness by thee blushing stand!
To be so tickled, they would change their state
And situation with those dancing chips,
O'er whom thy fingers walk with gentle gait,
Making dead wood more bless'd than living lips.
Since saucy jacks so happy are in this,
Give them thy fingers, me thy lips to kiss.

CXXIX

The expense of spirit in a waste of shame
Is lust in action: and till action, lust
Is perjured, murderous, bloody, full of blame,
Savage, extreme, rude, cruel, not to trust;
Enjoyed no sooner but despised straight;
Past reason hunted; and no sooner had,
Past reason hated, as a swallowed bait,
On purpose laid to make the taker mad.
Mad in pursuit and in possession so;
Had, having, and in quest to have extreme;
A bliss in proof, and proved, a very woe;
Before, a joy proposed; behind a dream.
All this the world well knows; yet none knows well
To shun the heaven that leads men to this hell.

CXXX

My mistress' eyes are nothing like the sun;
Coral is far more red, than her lips red:
If snow be white, why then her breasts are dun;
If hairs be wires, black wires grow on her head.
I have seen roses damasked, red and white,
But no such roses see I in her cheeks;
And in some perfumes is there more delight
Than in the breath that from my mistress reeks.
I love to hear her speak, yet well I know
That music hath a far more pleasing sound:
I grant I never saw a goddess go,
My mistress, when she walks, treads on the ground:
And yet by heaven, I think my love as rare,
As any she belied with false compare.

CXXXI

Thou art as tyrannous, so as thou art,
As those whose beauties proudly make them cruel;
For well thou know'st to my dear doting heart
Thou art the fairest and most precious jewel.
Yet, in good faith, some say that thee behold,
Thy face hath not the power to make love groan;
To say they err I dare not be so bold,
Although I swear it to myself alone.
And to be sure that is not false I swear,
A thousand groans, but thinking on thy face,
One on another's neck, do witness bear
Thy black is fairest in my judgment's place.
In nothing art thou black save in thy deeds,
And thence this slander, as I think, proceeds.

CXXXII

Thine eyes I love, and they, as pitying me,
Knowing thy heart torments me with disdain,
Have put on black and loving mourners be,
Looking with pretty ruth upon my pain.
And truly not the morning sun of heaven
Better becomes the grey cheeks of the east,
Nor that full star that ushers in the even,
Doth half that glory to the sober west,
As those two mourning eyes become thy face:
O! let it then as well beseem thy heart
To mourn for me since mourning doth thee grace,
And suit thy pity like in every part.
Then will I swear beauty herself is black,
And all they foul that thy complexion lack.

CXXXIII

Beshrew that heart that makes my heart to groan
For that deep wound it gives my friend and me!
Is't not enough to torture me alone,
But slave to slavery my sweet'st friend must be?
Me from myself thy cruel eye hath taken,
And my next self thou harder hast engrossed:
Of him, myself, and thee I am forsaken;
A torment thrice three-fold thus to be crossed.
Prison my heart in thy steel bosom's ward,
But then my friend's heart let my poor heart bail;
Whoe'er keeps me, let my heart be his guard;
Thou canst not then use rigour in my jail:
And yet thou wilt; for I, being pent in thee,
Perforce am thine, and all that is in me.

CXXXIV

So now I have confessed that he is thine,
And I my self am mortgaged to thy will,
Myself I'll forfeit, so that other mine
Thou wilt restore to be my comfort still:
But thou wilt not, nor he will not be free,
For thou art covetous, and he is kind;
He learned but surety-like to write for me,
Under that bond that him as fast doth bind.
The statute of thy beauty thou wilt take,
Thou usurer, that put'st forth all to use,
And sue a friend came debtor for my sake;
So him I lose through my unkind abuse.
Him have I lost; thou hast both him and me:
He pays the whole, and yet am I not free.

CXXXV

Whoever hath her wish, thou hast thy Will,
And Will to boot, and Will in over-plus;
More than enough am I that vexed thee still,
To thy sweet will making addition thus.
Wilt thou, whose will is large and spacious,
Not once vouchsafe to hide my will in thine?
Shall will in others seem right gracious,
And in my will no fair acceptance shine?
The sea, all water, yet receives rain still,
And in abundance addeth to his store;
So thou, being rich in Will, add to thy Will
One will of mine, to make thy large will more.
Let no unkind, no fair beseechers kill;
Think all but one, and me in that one Will.

CXXXVI

If thy soul check thee that I come so near,
Swear to thy blind soul that I was thy Will,
And will, thy soul knows, is admitted there;
Thus far for love, my love-suit, sweet, fulfil.
Will, will fulfil the treasure of thy love,
Ay, fill it full with wills, and my will one.
In things of great receipt with ease we prove
Among a number one is reckoned none:
Then in the number let me pass untold,
Though in thy store's account I one must be;
For nothing hold me, so it please thee hold
That nothing me, a something sweet to thee:
Make but my name thy love, and love that still,
And then thou lovest me for my name is 'Will.'

CXXXVII

Thou blind fool, Love, what dost thou to mine eyes,
That they behold, and see not what they see?
They know what beauty is, see where it lies,
Yet what the best is take the worst to be.
If eyes, corrupt by over-partial looks,
Be anchored in the bay where all men ride,
Why of eyes' falsehood hast thou forged hooks,
Whereto the judgment of my heart is tied?
Why should my heart think that a several plot,
Which my heart knows the wide world's common place?
Or mine eyes, seeing this, say this is not,
To put fair truth upon so foul a face?
In things right true my heart and eyes have erred,
And to this false plague are they now transferred.

CXXXVIII

When my love swears that she is made of truth,
I do believe her though I know she lies,
That she might think me some untutored youth,
Unlearned in the world's false subtleties.
Thus vainly thinking that she thinks me young,
Although she knows my days are past the best,
Simply I credit her false-speaking tongue:
On both sides thus is simple truth suppressed:
But wherefore says she not she is unjust?
And wherefore say not I that I am old?
O! love's best habit is in seeming trust,
And age in love, loves not to have years told:
Therefore I lie with her, and she with me,
And in our faults by lies we flattered be.

CXXXIX

O! call not me to justify the wrong
That thy unkindness lays upon my heart;
Wound me not with thine eye, but with thy tongue:
Use power with power, and slay me not by art,
Tell me thou lov'st elsewhere; but in my sight,
Dear heart, forbear to glance thine eye aside:
What need'st thou wound with cunning, when thy might
Is more than my o'erpressed defence can bide?
Let me excuse thee: ah! my love well knows
Her pretty looks have been mine enemies;
And therefore from my face she turns my foes,
That they elsewhere might dart their injuries:
Yet do not so; but since I am near slain,
Kill me outright with looks, and rid my pain.

CXL

Be wise as thou art cruel; do not press
My tongue-tied patience with too much disdain;
Lest sorrow lend me words, and words express
The manner of my pity-wanting pain.
If I might teach thee wit, better it were,
Though not to love, yet, love to tell me so;
As testy sick men, when their deaths be near,
No news but health from their physicians know;
For, if I should despair, I should grow mad,
And in my madness might speak ill of thee;
Now this ill-wresting world is grown so bad,
Mad slanderers by mad ears believed be.
That I may not be so, nor thou belied,
Bear thine eyes straight, though thy proud heart go wide.

CXLI

In faith I do not love thee with mine eyes,
For they in thee a thousand errors note;
But 'tis my heart that loves what they despise,
Who, in despite of view, is pleased to dote.
Nor are mine ears with thy tongue's tune delighted;
Nor tender feeling, to base touches prone,
Nor taste, nor smell, desire to be invited
To any sensual feast with thee alone:
But my five wits nor my five senses can
Dissuade one foolish heart from serving thee,
Who leaves unswayed the likeness of a man,
Thy proud heart's slave and vassal wretch to be:
Only my plague thus far I count my gain,
That she that makes me sin awards me pain.

CXLII

Love is my sin, and thy dear virtue hate,
Hate of my sin, grounded on sinful loving:
O! but with mine compare thou thine own state,
And thou shalt find it merits not reproving;
Or, if it do, not from those lips of thine,
That have profaned their scarlet ornaments
And sealed false bonds of love as oft as mine,
Robbed others' beds' revenues of their rents.
Be it lawful I love thee, as thou lov'st those
Whom thine eyes woo as mine importune thee:
Root pity in thy heart, that, when it grows,
Thy pity may deserve to pitied be.
If thou dost seek to have what thou dost hide,
By self-example mayst thou be denied!

CXLIII

Lo, as a careful housewife runs to catch
One of her feather'd creatures broke away,
Sets down her babe, and makes all swift dispatch
In pursuit of the thing she would have stay;
Whilst her neglected child holds her in chase,
Cries to catch her whose busy care is bent
To follow that which flies before her face,
Not prizing her poor infant's discontent;
So runn'st thou after that which flies from thee,
Whilst I thy babe chase thee afar behind;
But if thou catch thy hope, turn back to me,
And play the mother's part, kiss me, be kind;
So will I pray that thou mayst have thy 'Will,'
If thou turn back and my loud crying still.

CXLIV

Two loves I have of comfort and despair,
Which like two spirits do suggest me still:
The better angel is a man right fair,
The worser spirit a woman coloured ill.
To win me soon to hell, my female evil,
Tempteth my better angel from my side,
And would corrupt my saint to be a devil,
Wooing his purity with her foul pride.
And whether that my angel be turned fiend,
Suspect I may, yet not directly tell;
But being both from me, both to each friend,
I guess one angel in another's hell:
Yet this shall I ne'er know, but live in doubt,
Till my bad angel fire my good one out.

CXLV

Those lips that Love's own hand did make,
Breathed forth the sound that said 'I hate',
To me that languished for her sake:
But when she saw my woeful state,
Straight in her heart did mercy come,
Chiding that tongue that ever sweet
Was used in giving gentle doom;
And taught it thus anew to greet;
'I hate' she altered with an end,
That followed it as gentle day,
Doth follow night, who like a fiend
From heaven to hell is flown away.
'I hate', from hate away she threw,
And saved my life, saying 'not you'.

CXLVI

Poor soul, the centre of my sinful earth,
(???) these rebel powers that thee array,
Why dost thou pine within and suffer dearth,
Painting thy outward walls so costly gay?
Why so large cost, having so short a lease,
Dost thou upon thy fading mansion spend?
Shall worms, inheritors of this excess,
Eat up thy charge? Is this thy body's end?
Then soul, live thou upon thy servant's loss,
And let that pine to aggravate thy store;
Buy terms divine in selling hours of dross;
Within be fed, without be rich no more:
So shall thou feed on Death, that feeds on men,
And Death once dead, there's no more dying then.

CXLVII

My love is as a fever longing still,
For that which longer nurseth the disease;
Feeding on that which doth preserve the ill,
The uncertain sickly appetite to please.
My reason, the physician to my love,
Angry that his prescriptions are not kept,
Hath left me, and I desperate now approve
Desire is death, which physic did except.
Past cure I am, now Reason is past care,
And frantic-mad with evermore unrest;
My thoughts and my discourse as madmen's are,
At random from the truth vainly expressed;
For I have sworn thee fair, and thought thee bright,
Who art as black as hell, as dark as night.

CXLVIII

O me! what eyes hath Love put in my head,
Which have no correspondence with true sight;
Or, if they have, where is my judgment fled,
That censures falsely what they see aright?
If that be fair whereon my false eyes dote,
What means the world to say it is not so?
If it be not, then love doth well denote
Love's eye is not so true as all men's: no,
How can it? O! how can Love's eye be true,
That is so vexed with watching and with tears?
No marvel then, though I mistake my view;
The sun itself sees not, till heaven clears.
O cunning Love! with tears thou keep'st me blind,
Lest eyes well-seeing thy foul faults should find.

CXLIX

Canst thou, O cruel! say I love thee not,
When I against myself with thee partake?
Do I not think on thee, when I forgot
Am of my self, all tyrant, for thy sake?
Who hateth thee that I do call my friend,
On whom frown'st thou that I do fawn upon,
Nay, if thou lour'st on me, do I not spend
Revenge upon myself with present moan?
What merit do I in my self respect,
That is so proud thy service to despise,
When all my best doth worship thy defect,
Commanded by the motion of thine eyes?
But, love, hate on, for now I know thy mind,
Those that can see thou lov'st, and I am blind.

CL

O! from what power hast thou this powerful might,
With insufficiency my heart to sway?
To make me give the lie to my true sight,
And swear that brightness doth not grace the day?
Whence hast thou this becoming of things ill,
That in the very refuse of thy deeds
There is such strength and warrantise of skill,
That, in my mind, thy worst all best exceeds?
Who taught thee how to make me love thee more,
The more I hear and see just cause of hate?
O! though I love what others do abhor,
With others thou shouldst not abhor my state:
If thy unworthiness raised love in me,
More worthy I to be beloved of thee.

CLI

Love is too young to know what conscience is,
Yet who knows not conscience is born of love?
Then, gentle cheater, urge not my amiss,
Lest guilty of my faults thy sweet self prove:
For, thou betraying me, I do betray
My nobler part to my gross body's treason;
My soul doth tell my body that he may
Triumph in love; flesh stays no farther reason,
But rising at thy name doth point out thee,
As his triumphant prize. Proud of this pride,
He is contented thy poor drudge to be,
To stand in thy affairs, fall by thy side.
No want of conscience hold it that I call
Her love, for whose dear love I rise and fall.

CLII

In loving thee thou know'st I am forsworn,
But thou art twice forsworn, to me love swearing;
In act thy bed-vow broke, and new faith torn,
In vowing new hate after new love bearing:
But why of two oaths' breach do I accuse thee,
When I break twenty? I am perjured most;
For all my vows are oaths but to misuse thee,
And all my honest faith in thee is lost:
For I have sworn deep oaths of thy deep kindness,
Oaths of thy love, thy truth, thy constancy;
And, to enlighten thee, gave eyes to blindness,
Or made them swear against the thing they see;
For I have sworn thee fair; more perjured eye,
To swear against the truth so foul a lie!

CLIII

Cupid laid by his brand and fell asleep:
A maid of Dian's this advantage found,
And his love-kindling fire did quickly steep
In a cold valley-fountain of that ground;
Which borrowed from this holy fire of Love,
A dateless lively heat, still to endure,
And grew a seething bath, which yet men prove
Against strange maladies a sovereign cure.
But at my mistress' eye Love's brand new-fired,
The boy for trial needs would touch my breast;
I, sick withal, the help of bath desired,
And thither hied, a sad distempered guest,
But found no cure, the bath for my help lies
Where Cupid got new fire; my mistress' eyes.

CLIV

The little Love-god lying once asleep,
Laid by his side his heart-inflaming brand,
Whilst many nymphs that vowed chaste life to keep
Came tripping by; but in her maiden hand
The fairest votary took up that fire
Which many legions of true hearts had warmed;
And so the General of hot desire
Was, sleeping, by a virgin hand disarmed.
This brand she quenched in a cool well by,
Which from Love's fire took heat perpetual,
Growing a bath and healthful remedy,
For men diseased; but I, my mistress' thrall,
Came there for cure and this by that I prove,
Love's fire heats water, water cools not love.

Sonnets Xxix: When, In Disgrace With Fortune And Men's Eyes

When, in disgrace with fortune and men's eyes,
I all alone beweep my outcast state
And trouble deaf heaven with my bootless cries
And look upon myself and curse my fate,
Wishing me like to one more rich in hope,
Featur'd like him, like him with friends possess'd,
Desiring this man's art and that man's scope,
With what I most enjoy contented least;
Yet in these thoughts myself almost despising,
Haply I think on thee, and then my state,
Like to the lark at break of day arising
From sullen earth, sings hymns at heaven's gate;
For thy sweet love remember'd such wealth brings
That then I scorn to change my state with kings.

Sonnets Xciv: They That Have Power To Hurt And Will Do None

They that have power to hurt and will do none,
That do not do the thing they most do show,
Who, moving others, are themselves as stone,
Unmoved, cold, and to temptation slow:
They rightly do inherit heaven's graces
And husband nature's riches from expense;
They are the lords and owners of their faces,
Others but stewards of their excellence.
The summer's flower is to the summer sweet
Though to itself it only live and die,
But if that flower with base infection meet,
The basest weed outbraves his dignity:
For sweetest things turn sourest by their deeds;
Lilies that fester smell far worse than weeds.

Helen's Soliloqy (All's Well That Ends Well)

Our remedies oft in ourselves do lie
Which we ascribe to heaven. The fated sky
Gives us free scope, only doth backward pull
Our slow designs when we ourselves are dull.
What power is it which mounts my love so high,
That makes me see, and cannot feed mine eye?
The mightiest space in fortune nature brings
To join like likes and kiss like native things.
Impossible be strange attempts to those
That weigh their pains in sense and do suppose
What hath been cannot be. Who ever strove
To show her merit that did miss her love?

Sonnets Vii

BEING your slave, what should I do but tend
Upon the hours and times of your desire?
I have no precious time at all to spend,
Nor services to do, till you require.
Nor dare I chide the world-without-end hour
Whilst I, my sovereign, watch the clock for you,
Nor think the bitterness of absence sour
When you have bid your servant once adieu;
Nor dare I question with my jealous thought
Where you may be, or your affairs suppose,
But, like a sad slave, stay and think of nought
Save, where you are how happy you make those!
So true a fool is love, that in your Will,
Though you do any thing, he thinks no ill.

Sonnets Xiv

MY love is strengthen'd, though more weak in seeming;
I love not less, though less the show appear:
That love is merchandised whose rich esteeming
The owner's tongue doth publish everywhere.
Our love was new, and then but in the spring,
When I was wont to greet it with my lays;
As Philomel in summer's front doth sing
And stops her pipe in growth of riper days:
Not that the summer is less pleasant now
Than when her mournful hymns did hush the night,
But that wild music burthens every bough,
And sweets grown common lose their dear delight.
Therefore, like her, I sometime hold my tongue,
Because I would not dull you with my song.

Antony and Cleopatra, Act II, Scene II [The barge she sat in, like a burnish'd throne]

Enobarbus describes Queen Cleopatra
Enobarbus: I will tell you.
The barge she sat in, like a burnish'd throne,
Burned on the water: the poop was beaten gold;
Purple the sails, and so perfumed that
The winds were lovesick with them; the oars were silver,
Which to the tune of flutes kept stroke, and made
The water which they beat to follow faster,
As amorous of their strokes. For her own person,
It beggar'd all description: she did lie
In her pavilion, cloth-of-gold of tissue,
O'erpicturing that Venus where we see
The fancy outwork nature: on each side her
Stood pretty dimpled boys, like smiling Cupids,
With divers-colour'd fans, whose wind did seem
To glow the delicate cheeks which they did cool,
And what they undid did.

Agrippa: O, rare for Antony.

Enobarbus: Her gentlewomen, like the Nereides,
So many mermaids, tended her i' th' eyes,
And made their bends adornings. At the helm
A seeming mermaid steers: the silken tackle
Swell with the touches of those flower-soft hands
That yarely frame the office. From the barge
A strange invisible perfume hits the sense
Of the adjacent wharfs. The city cast
Her people out upon her; and Antony,
Enthroned i' th' marketplace, did sit alone,
Whistling to th' air; which, but for vacancy,
Had gone to gaze on Cleopatra too,
And made a gap in nature.

Agrippa: Rare Egyptian!

Enobarbus: Upon her landing, Antony sent to her,
Invited her to supper. She replied
It should be better he became her guest;
Which she entreated. Our courteous Antony,
Whom ne'er the word of "No" woman heard speak,
Being barbered ten times o'er, goes to the feast,
And for his ordinary, pays his heart
For what his eyes eat only.

Agrippa: Royal wench!
She made great Caesar lay his sword to bed;
He plowed her, and she cropped.

Enobarbus: I saw her once
Hop forty paces through the public street;
And having lost her breath, she spoke, and panted,
That she did make defect perfection,
And, breathless, pow'r breathe forth.

Maecenas: Now Antony must leave her utterly.

Enobarbus: Never; He will not:
Age cannot wither her, nor custom stale
Her infinite variety. Other women cloy
The appetites they feed, but she makes hungry
Where most she satisfies; for vilest things
Become themselves in her, that the holy priests
Bless her when she is riggish.

Sonnets Xviii

LET me not to the marriage of true minds
Admit impediments. Love is not love
Which alters when it alteration finds,
Or bends with the remover to remove:
O, no! it is an ever-fixed mark,
That looks on tempests and is never shaken;
It is the star to every wand'ring bark,
Whose worth 's unknown, although his height be taken.
Love 's not Time's fool, though rosy lips and cheeks
Within his bending sickle's compass come;
Love alters not with his brief hours and weeks,
But bears it out even to the edge of doom:--
If this be error and upon me proved,
I never writ, nor no man ever loved.

Sonnet Lxx

That thou art blamed shall not be thy defect,
For slander's mark was ever yet the fair;
The ornament of beauty is suspect,
A crow that flies in heaven's sweetest air.
So thou be good, slander doth but approve
Thy worth the greater, being woo'd of time;
For canker vice the sweetest buds doth love,
And thou present'st a pure unstained prime.
Thou hast pass'd by the ambush of young days,
Either not assail'd or victor being charged;
Yet this thy praise cannot be so thy praise,
To tie up envy evermore enlarged:
If some suspect of ill mask'd not thy show,
Then thou alone kingdoms of hearts shouldst owe.